D0130247

$\mathcal{L}$ENT *and*
$\mathcal{E}$ASTER
$\mathcal{W}$ISDOM
from
SAINT IGNATIUS OF LOYOLA

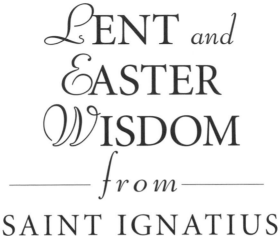

Lent and Easter Wisdom
from
SAINT IGNATIUS
OF LOYOLA

Daily Scripture and Prayers
Together With Saint Ignatius' Own Words

Compiled by James L. Connor, SJ

Liguori
LIGUORI, MISSOURI

Imprimi Potest:
Thomas D. Picton, C.Ss.R.
Provincial, Denver Province
The Redemptorists

Published by Liguori
Liguori, Missouri
To order, call 800–325–9521.
www.liguori.org

Library of Congress Cataloging-in-Publication Data
Ignatius, of Loyola, Saint, 1491-1556.
   [Selections. English. 2009]
   Lent and Easter wisdom from Saint Ignatius of Loyola / compiled by James L. Connor.—1st ed.
   p. cm.
   ISBN 978-0-7648-1821-9
   1. Lent—Prayers and devotions. 2. Easter—Prayers and devotions. 3. Catholic Church—Prayers and devotions. I. Connor, James L. II. Title.
   BX2170.L4I38 2009
   242'.34—dc22

2009035574

Printed in the United States of America
First edition
13 12 11 10 09 5 4 3 2 1

Contents

Introduction

BORN IN OCTOBER 1491, IGNATIUS WAS the youngest of the thirteen children of a Basque nobleman of the ancient and well-to-do family of Loyola. At the age of sixteen, Ignatius was sent to be a page in the court of the treasurer at the kingdom of Castille. Prone to vanity, he became, on his own admission, addicted to gambling, sword play, and women. When he was thirty-one, he was severely wounded in battle. During his long recuperation, while reading a Life of Christ and a book of the lives of the saints, he underwent a profound religious conversion. From that time on, he dedicated his life to companionship with Jesus in his mission of serving others. As soon as he was well enough, he journeyed to Jerusalem in order to walk in Jesus' footsteps. On returning to Europe, he enrolled in school where he led a group of friends through the steps of his own conversion experience—soon to be called his "Spiritual Exercises"—and with them, founded a religious order, The Companions (or Society) of Jesus. Their mission was to "save souls" by directing others in the Spiritual Exercises, preaching, teaching, and serving the poor. During Lent and Easter week, we will be walking with Jesus under the guidance of Saint Ignatius of Loyola and his Spiritual Exercises.

On the first thirteen days of our journey, we will accompany Saint Ignatius Loyola as he makes his own Lent-to-Easter journey in a personal conversion experience under the guidance of Jesus. Thereafter, we will be guided by Saint Ignatius along the pathway of his Spiritual Exercises on our own Lent-to-Easter journey with Christ.

A BRIEF HISTORY OF LENT

Most Catholics seem to be aware that the forty-day period before the feast of Easter—Lent, which comes from the Anglo-Saxon word *lencten*, meaning "spring"—is a time marked by particular rituals such as the reception of ashes on Ash Wednesday or the decision to give up French fries. Is Lent broader than just these practices that seem to be left over from another era?

In the first three centuries of Christian experience, preparation for the Easter feast usually covered a period of one or two days, perhaps a week at the most. Saint Irenaeus of Lyons (ca. AD 140–202) even speaks of a *forty-hour* preparation for Easter.

The first reference to Lent as a period of forty days' preparation occurs in the teachings of the First Council of Nicaea in AD 325. By the end of the fourth century, a Lenten period of forty days was established and accepted.

In its early development, Lent quickly became associated with the sacrament of baptism, since Easter was the great baptismal feast. Those who were preparing to be baptized participated in the season of Lent in preparation for the reception of the sacrament of baptism. Eventually, those who were already baptized considered it important to join these candidates preparing for baptism in their preparations for Easter. The customs and practices of Lent as we know them today soon took hold.

LENT AS A JOURNEY

Lent is often portrayed as a journey, from one point in time to another point in time. The concept of journey is obvious for those experiencing the Rite of Christian Initiation of Adults (RCIA), the program of baptismal preparation conducted in most parishes during the season of Lent.

But Lenten preparation is not limited to those who are preparing to be baptized and join the Church. For many Catholics, Lent is a journey that is measured from Ash Wednesday through Easter Sunday, but more accurately, Lent is measured from Ash Wednesday to the beginning of the period known as the Triduum.

Triduum begins with the Mass on Holy Thursday, continues through Good Friday, and concludes with the Easter Vigil on Holy Saturday. Triduum officially ends with the proclamation of the Exsultet, "Rejoice, O Heavenly Powers," during the Mass of Holy Saturday.

By whatever yardstick the journey is measured, it is not only the time that is important but the essential experiences of the journey that are necessary for a full appreciation of what is being celebrated.

The Lenten journey is also a process of spiritual growth and, as such, presumes movement from one state of being to another state. For example, some people may find themselves troubled and anxious at the beginning of Lent as a result of a life choice or an unanswered question, and, at the end of Lent, they may fully expect a sense of conversion, a sense of peace, or perhaps simply understanding and acceptance. Therefore, Lent is a movement from one point of view to another or, perhaps, from one interpretation of life to a different interpretation.

Scripture, psalms, prayers, rituals, practices, and penance are the components of the Lenten journey. Each component, tried and tested by years of tradition, is one of the "engines" that drives the season and which brings the weary spiritual traveler to the joys of Easter.

PENITENTIAL NATURE OF LENT

A popular understanding of Lent is that it is a penitential period of time during which people attempt to become more sensitive to the role of sin in their lives. Lenten sermons will speak of personal sin, coming to an awareness of the sins of others and the effect such sin might have, and the sin that can be found within our larger society and culture. Awareness of sin, however, is balanced by an emphasis on the love and acceptance that God still has for humanity, despite the sinful condition in which we still find ourselves.

The practice of meditation of the Passion of the Lord, his suffering and his death, is also seen as part of the penitential experience of Lent. There is also a traditional concern for the reception of the sacrament of reconciliation during Lent. Originally, the sacrament of reconciliation was celebrated before Lent began. The penance was imposed on Ash Wednesday and performed during the entire forty-day period.

SUMMONS TO PENITENTIAL LIVING

"Jesus came to Galilee, proclaiming the good news of God, and saying, 'The time is fulfilled, and the kingdom of God has come near; repent, and believe in the good news'" (Mark 1:14–15). This call to conversion announces the solemn opening of Lent. Participants are marked with ashes, and the words, "Repent, and believe in the good news," are prayed. This blessing is understood as a personal acceptance of the desire to take on the life of penance for the sake of the Gospel.

The example of Jesus in the desert for forty days—a time during which he fasted and prayed—is imitated. It is time to center attention on conversion. During Lent, the expectation is to examine our lives and, through the practice of prayer, fasting, and works of charity, seek to conform our lives to Christ's. For some, this conversion will be a turning from sin to grace. For others, it will be a gracious turning toward the mystery of God in Christ. Whatever the pattern chosen by a particular pilgrim for an observance of Lent, it is hoped that this book will provide a useful support in the effort.

PART I

READINGS for LENT

DAY 1

The Lenten Journey Begins

IGNATIUS WRITES OF HIMSELF

*U*p to his twenty-sixth year he was a man given over to the vanities of the world, and took a special delight in the exercise of arms, with a great and vain desire of winning glory. He was in a fortress which the French were attacking....After the assault had been going on for some time, a cannon ball struck him in the leg, crushing its bones, and because it passed between his legs it also seriously wounded the other....

After twelve or fifteen days in Pamplona they bore him in a litter to his own country.

ST. IGNATIUS' OWN STORY (WRITTEN IN THIRD PERSON), 7

SAINT PAUL'S CALL TO CONVERSION

Meanwhile Saul, still breathing threats and murder against the disciples of the Lord, went to the high priest and asked him for letters to the synagogues at Damascus, so that if he found any who belonged to the Way, men or women, he might bring them bound to Jerusalem. Now as he was going along and approaching Damascus, suddenly a light from heaven flashed around him. He fell to the ground and heard a voice saying to him, "Saul, Saul, why do you persecute me?" He asked, "Who are you, Lord?" The reply came, "I am Jesus, whom you are persecuting."

ACTS 9:1–5

PRAYER

Dear Lord, as you called Saint Paul and Saint Ignatius to a profound conversion to serve your people, please give me the generosity to respond to your call during this Lenten and Easter celebration.

LENTEN ACTION

Jot down two things today in the journal you are keeping during this Lent and Easter experience:
- What blocks you from being attentive and responsive to the needs of others?
- Describe the joy you experienced when you helped someone who was really in need.

DAY 2

God's Providence in Life Experiences

THE POWER OF VANITY

When the bones knit, one below the knee remained astride another, which caused a shortening of the leg. The bones so raised cause a protuberance that was not pleasant to the sight. The sick man was not able to put up with this, because he had made up his mind to seek his fortune in the world. He…asked the surgeons whether it could not be cut away. They told him that it could be cut away, but that the pain would be greater than all he had already suffered….He determined, nevertheless, to undergo this martyrdom to gratify his own inclinations.

ST. IGNATIUS' OWN STORY, 8

THE POWER OF SERVICE

"A certain Ananias, who was a devout man according to the law and well spoken of by all the Jews living there, came to me; and standing beside me, he said, 'Brother Saul, regain your sight!' In that very hour I regained my sight and saw him. Then he said, 'The God of our ancestors has chosen you to know his will, to see the Righteous One and to hear his own voice; for you will be his witness to all the world of what you have seen and heard.'"

ACTS 22:12–15

PRAYER

Dear Lord, as I embark on this Lenten and Easter journey, free me from the vanity that imprisoned the young Ignatius Loyola. Fill me with the Holy Spirit that empowered Paul of Tarsus to travel the known world in service of others and the call of the Gospel. This I ask in the name of Jesus our Lord. Amen.

LENTEN ACTION

Look for the opportunity throughout the day to congratulate at least two people for something they have done well. Nothing builds trust and confidence more than affirmation like that.

DAY 3

FRIDAY AFTER ASH WEDNESDAY

The Beginnings of a Call

THE CHRIST LIFE: THE MESSAGE

He had been much given to reading worldly books of fiction and knight errantry, and feeling well enough to read he asked for some of these books to help while away the time. In that house, however, they could find none of those he was accustomed to read, and so they gave him a Life of Christ and a book of the Lives of the Saints in Spanish.

By the frequent reading of these books he conceived some affection for what he found there narrated. Pausing in his reading, he gave himself up to thinking over what he had read.

ST. IGNATIUS' OWN STORY, 8

THE CHRIST-LIFE: THE MISSION

"But get up and stand on your feet; for I have appeared to you for this purpose, to appoint you to serve and testify to the things in which you have seen me and to those in which I will appear to you. I will rescue you from your people and from the Gentiles—to whom I am sending you to open their eyes so that they may turn from darkness to light and from the power of Satan to God, so that they may receive forgiveness of sins and a place among those who are sanctified by faith in me."

ACTS 26:16–18

PRAYER

Dear Lord, let the young Ignatius be my model when I read or hear the Gospel story of Jesus and his life. Help me to read slowly, to pause and reflect, and to appreciate gratefully what Jesus has done for me and the life he has given me. This I pray through Christ our Lord. Amen.

LENTEN ACTION

Jot down briefly in your Lent and Easter journal three incidents in the life of Jesus that really move you. Describe—again briefly—why you find them so moving. Say a short prayer of thanks to Jesus.

DAY 4

Growing Up to Childhood

THE MAN OF THE WORLD

*A*t other times, he dwelt on the things of the world which formerly had occupied his thoughts. Of the many vain things that presented themselves to him, one took such possession of his heart that without realizing it he could spend two, three, or even four hours on end thinking of it, fancying what he would have to do in the service of a certain lady, of the means he would take to reach the country where she was living, of the verses, the promises he would make her, the deeds of gallantry he would do in her service.

ST. IGNATIUS' OWN STORY, 9

THE CHILD OF GOD

At that time the disciples came to Jesus and asked, "Who is the greatest in the kingdom of heaven?" He called a child, whom he put among them, and said, "Truly I tell you, unless you change and become like children, you will never enter the kingdom of heaven. Whoever becomes humble like this child is the greatest in the kingdom of heaven. Whoever welcomes one such child in my name welcomes me."

MATTHEW 18:1–5

PRAYER

Dear Lord, show me how I can help others realize their true greatness, not as self-promoting "men of the world," but as humble children of God. This I pray in the name of Jesus the Lord. Amen.

LENTEN ACTION

Can you think of a person (perhaps someone you know personally) who is really accomplished, admittedly a leader, and very successful—but who is, at heart, a very childlike individual: humble, simple, and appreciative of others? Ponder that person. What makes him or her "tick"?

DAY 5

Motivation

"I MUST DO IT!"

*I*n reading the Life of our Lord and the Lives of the Saints, he paused to think and reason with himself. "Suppose that I should do what St. Francis did, what St. Dominic did?" He thus let his thoughts run over many things that seemed good to him, always putting before himself things that were difficult and important which seemed to him easy to accomplish when he proposed them. But all his thought was to tell himself, "St. Dominic did this, therefore, I must do it. St. Francis did this; therefore, I must do it." These thoughts also lasted a good while.

ST. IGNATIUS' OWN STORY, 9

"DO EVERYTHING FOR THE GLORY OF GOD"

[W]hether you eat or drink, or whatever you do, do everything for the glory of God. Give no offence to Jews or to Greeks or to the church of God, just as I try to please everyone in everything I do, not seeking my own advantage, but that of many, so that they may be saved. Be imitators of me, as I am of Christ.

1 CORINTHIANS 10:31–11:1

PRAYER

Lord, help me to be like you in my actions, my aspirations, and my affections. Help me to see the activities of this day through your eyes. Help me to live this day in a way that pleases you. Amen.

LENTEN ACTION

Consciously offer your day today for the greater glory of God. Choose your activities, your speech, and your attitudes by considering what Jesus Christ and your favorite saint would do in your situation.

DAY 6

Two Spirits

THE SPIRIT OF EVIL AND THE SPIRIT OF GOD

*W*hen he was thinking of the things of the world he was filled with delight, but when afterwards he dismissed them from weariness, he was dry and dissatisfied. And when he thought of going barefoot to Jerusalem and...the other rigors...that the Saints had performed, he was consoled, not only when he entertained these thoughts, but even after dismissing them he remained cheerful and satisfied....[O]ne day his eyes were opened a little....[H]e came to recognize the difference between the two spirits that moved him, the one being from the evil spirit, the other from God.

ST. IGNATIUS' OWN STORY, 10

LIVE BY THE SPIRIT!

Live by the Spirit, I say, and do not gratify the desires of the flesh. For what the flesh desires is opposed to the Spirit, and what the Spirit desires is opposed to the flesh; for these are opposed to each other, to prevent you from doing what you want. But if you are led by the Spirit, you are not subject to the law. Now the works of the flesh are obvious....

By contrast, the fruit of the Spirit is love, joy, peace, patience, kindness, generosity, faithfulness, gentleness, and self-control. There is no law against such things. And those who belong to Christ Jesus have crucified the flesh with its passions and desires. If we live by the Spirit, let us also be guided by the Spirit.

GALATIANS 5:16–25

PRAYER

Dear God, you know how many times I live my life based upon my feelings—and how often my choices are a result of laziness, selfishness, or fear. I want to live in truth and love. Please show me the way. I ask this in the name of Christ the Lord. Amen.

ACTION

Twice today—once in the morning and once in the afternoon—stop and reflect: "How am I feeling?" Name your feeling(s). Then ask, "Are they saying something to me?" "Is there something they—and God—are asking me to do?"

DAY 7

Conversion of Heart

NEED FOR REPENTANCE

He acquired no little light from this reading and began to think more seriously of his past life and the great need he had of doing penance for it. It was during this reading that these desires of imitating the saints came to him, but with no further thought of circumstances than of promising to do with God's grace what they had done. What he desired most of all to do, as soon as he was restored to health, was to go to Jerusalem...undertaking all the disciplines and abstinences which a generous soul on fire with the love of God is wont to desire.

ST. IGNATIUS' OWN STORY, 10

"Prepare the Way of the Lord"

In those days John the Baptist appeared in the wilderness of Judea, proclaiming, "Repent, for the kingdom of heaven has come near." This is the one of whom the prophet Isaiah spoke when he said, "The voice of one crying out in the wilderness:
'Prepare the way of the Lord,
make his paths straight.'"

MATTHEW 3:1–3

Prayer

Jesus, John the Baptist prepared the way for you. Help me, this Lent, to be like John the Baptist, preparing your way to come into my heart, my family, and the world. Like Saint Ignatius, I want to learn to love you with all my heart, mind, and spirit. I ask this in your holy name. Amen.

Lenten Action

Write down a list of the things people do when they are in love with someone. Go over the list and identify one or two things on the list that apply to your growing relationship of love with God. Practice doing these things each day during Lent.

DAY 8

A New Future

CONSOLATION AND REGRET

One night, as he lay awake, he saw clearly the likeness of our Lady with the holy Child Jesus, at the sight of which he received most abundant consolation for a considerable interval of time. He felt so great a disgust with his past life, especially with its offenses of the flesh, that he thought all such images which had formerly occupied his mind were wiped out....[H]is brother and other members of the family easily recognized the change that had taken place in the interior of his soul from what they saw in his outward manner.

ST. IGNATIUS' OWN STORY, 11

JOY IN FORGIVENESS

Happy are those whose transgression is forgiven,
whose sin is covered.
Happy are those to whom the Lord imputes no iniquity,
and in whose spirit there is no deceit....
Then I acknowledged my sin to you,
and I did not hide my iniquity;
I said, 'I will confess my transgressions to the Lord,'
and you forgave the guilt of my sin.
Therefore let all who are faithful
offer prayer to you;...
[S]teadfast love surrounds those who trust in the Lord.
Be glad in the Lord and rejoice, O righteous,
and shout for joy, all you upright in heart.

PSALM 32

PRAYER

Lord, so often I justify my sins and make excuses for the reasons I have done what I ought not to have done. I know that you see me with all of my virtues and my vices. I thank you for loving me as I am, and yet challenging me to become more. Help me to have clear eyes and a penitent heart. This I ask in the name of Christ the Lord. Amen.

LENTEN ACTION

Imagine that you are standing before Jesus on the last day of your life. What does He say to you? Give thanks for the things you have done well, and ask for forgiveness for times when you chose your kingdom rather than his.

DAY 9

A New Journey

THE URGE TO SERVE

*I*t was his greatest consolation to gaze upon the heavens and the stars, which he often did, and for long stretches at a time, because when doing so he felt within himself a powerful urge to be serving our Lord. He gave much time to thinking about his resolve, desiring to be entirely well so that he could begin his journey [to Jerusalem].

…Indeed, feeling that he was pretty well restored, he thought it was time to be up and going and told his brother so.

ST. IGNATIUS' OWN STORY, 11–12

BLESS THE LORD!

Bless the Lord, all you works of the Lord,
praise and exalt him above all forever.
Angels of the Lord, bless the Lord,...
You heavens, bless the Lord,...
All you waters above the heavens, bless the Lord,...
All you hosts of the Lord, bless the Lord,...
Sun and moon, bless the Lord,...
Stars of heaven, bless the Lord,...
Light and darkness, bless the Lord,...
Lightnings and clouds, bless the Lord,...
Let the earth bless the Lord,
praise and exalt him above all forever.

DANIEL 3:57–63, 72–74 (*NAB*)

PRAYER

Lord, as I gaze at the heavens—the sky and the stars—help me to feel your presence in the expansiveness of the universe. And help me to hear your call to serve your people. Give me the generosity to do so courageously, for without you I can do nothing. Amen.

LENTEN ACTION

Take a leisurely walk; notice the beauty of the earth and the wonder of life. Give thanks for all that comes from the hand of God.

DAY 10

Preparing for Service

TAKING OFF THE "OLD MAN" AND PUTTING ON THE "NEW"

*H*e continued his way to Montserrat, thinking as usual of the great deeds he was going to do for the love of God....He determined, therefore, on a watch of arms throughout a whole night, without ever sitting or lying down, but standing a while and then kneeling, before the altar of our Lady of Montserrat, where he had made up his mind to leave his fine attire and to clothe himself with the armor of Christ....[A]fter praying for a while and making an engagement with his confessor, he made a general confession in writing which lasted three days.

ST. IGNATIUS' OWN STORY, 15

The Belt of Truth—The Shield of Faith

Put on the whole armour of God, so that you may be able to stand against the wiles of the devil. For our struggle is not against enemies of blood and flesh, but against the rulers, against the authorities, against the cosmic powers of this present darkness, against the spiritual forces of evil in the heavenly places. Therefore take up the whole armour of God, so that you may be able to withstand on that evil day, and having done everything, to stand firm. Stand therefore, and fasten the belt of truth around your waist, and put on the breastplate of righteousness. As shoes for your feet put on whatever will make you ready to proclaim the gospel of peace. With all of these, take the shield of faith, with which you will be able to quench all the flaming arrows of the evil one. Take the helmet of salvation, and the sword of the Spirit, which is the word of God.

Ephesians 6:11–17

Prayer

Dear Lord, by giving his sword to your Blessed Mother, Saint Ignatius trusted that she would guide him to you. Mary, guide me to Jesus. Please pray that I may develop a spirit like Saint Ignatius—one that is both contemplative and conquering. This I ask in the name of Christ the Lord. Amen.

Lenten Action

Strive to be both contemplative and conquering today. What is it that you need to gain the strength to do? Spend some time reflecting on the things you sense the Lord is calling you to do. Write them down in your journal.

DAY 11

Hearing the Word of the Lord

GOD THE TEACHER

*A*t this time God treated him just as a schoolmaster treats a little boy when he teaches him. This perhaps was because of his rough and uncultivated understanding, or because he had no one to teach him, or because of the firm will God Himself had given him in His service. But he clearly saw, and always had seen that God dealt with him like this. Rather, he thought that any doubt about it would be an offense against His Divine Majesty.

ST. IGNATIUS' OWN STORY, 22

REVEALED TO "INFANTS"

At that time Jesus said, "I thank you, Father, Lord of heaven and earth, because you have hidden these things from the wise and the intelligent and have revealed them to infants; yes, Father, for such was your gracious will. All things have been handed over to me by my Father; and no one knows the Son except the Father, and no one knows the Father except the Son and anyone to whom the Son chooses to reveal him."

MATTHEW 11:25–27

PRAYER

Lord, I am a child in need of your wisdom. As you instructed Saint Ignatius of Loyola, teach me your ways and guide me to know, love, and live in truth. This I ask in the name of Jesus the Lord. Amen.

LENTEN ACTION

Read Mother Mary's beautiful prayer, The Magnificat, in Luke 1:47–55. Notice especially the words: "…he has looked with favor on the lowliness of his servant," and "the Mighty One has done great things for me." Jot down in your journal the ways in which you are God's "lowly servant" and pray to feel joy!

DAY 12

From Experience to Expression

THE SPIRITUAL EXERCISES

*T*he Exercises were not composed all at one time, but things that he had observed in his own soul and found useful and which he thought would be useful to others, he put into writing—the examination of conscience, for example....The forms of [making] the election in particular, he told me, came from that variety of movement of spirits and thoughts which he experienced at Loyola, while he was still convalescing from his shattered leg.

ST. IGNATIUS' OWN STORY, 69

The Lord Counsels; The Soul Instructs

I bless the Lord who gives me counsel;
in the night also my heart instructs me.
I keep the Lord always before me;
because he is at my right hand, I shall not be moved.

Therefore my heart is glad, and my soul rejoices;
my body also rests secure.
You show me the path of life.
In your presence there is fullness of joy;
in your right hand are pleasures for evermore.

PSALM 16:7–9, 11

Prayer

Lord, I am so impatient with the process of becoming the person I was created to be. I want to be perfect—right now! Help me to recognize that life is a process of becoming, and that by following you, I will find myself. Amen.

Lenten Action

What things have given you the most assistance in your spiritual growth? Is there an event that served as a catalyst? Is there a person who inspired you? Write these things in your journal and give thanks for the process of becoming all that you are created to be.

DAY 13

Learning by Doing

SPIRITUAL EXERCISES: WHAT ARE THEY?

*B*y the term "Spiritual Exercises" is meant every method of examination of conscience, of meditation, of contemplation, of vocal and mental prayer, and of other spiritual activities that will be mentioned later. For just as taking a walk, journeying on foot, and running are bodily exercises, so we call Spiritual Exercises every way of preparing and disposing the soul to rid itself of all inordinate attachments, and, after their removal, of seeking and finding the will of God in the disposition of our life for the salvation of our soul.

THE SPIRITUAL EXERCISES OF ST. IGNATIUS
"INTRODUCTORY OBSERVATIONS," 1

RUN TO WIN!

Do you not know that in a race the runners all compete, but only one receives the prize? Run in such a way that you may win it. Athletes exercise self-control in all things; they do it to receive a perishable garland, but we an imperishable one. So I do not run aimlessly, nor do I box as though beating the air; but I punish my body and enslave it, so that after proclaiming to others I myself should not be disqualified.

1 CORINTHIANS 9:24–27

PRAYER

Dear Lord, I have never much thought of the spiritual life as exercise! Help me to run the race well, with my eye on the goal of life with you—in this world and the next. Saint Ignatius, please pray that I will have the discipline to persevere! In the name of Christ the Lord, Amen.

LENTEN ACTION

Take a walk or run today, and with each breath you take, be aware that you are breathing in God's presence. As you exhale, let go of selfishness and fear. Give thanks that God continually sustains your life.

DAY 14

The Exercises Begin: The First "Exercise"

WHO WE ARE BY GOD'S LOVING DESIRE AND DECISION

*M*an is created to praise, reverence, and serve God our Lord, and by this means to save his soul.

The other things on the face of the earth are created for man to help him in attaining the end for which he is created.

Hence, man is to make use of them in as far as they help him in the attainment of his end, and he must rid himself of them in as far as they prove a hindrance to him.

…Our one desire and choice should be what is more conducive to the end for which we are created.

SPIRITUAL EXERCISE, NO. 23
THE SPIRITUAL EXERCISES OF ST. IGNATIUS, 12

THY KINGDOM COME!

"Pray then in this way:
Our Father in heaven,
hallowed be your name.
Your kingdom come.
Your will be done,
on earth as it is in heaven."

MATTHEW 6:9–10

PRAYER

Dear Lord, I know that you want your kingdom to begin in my heart, extend to my friends, family, neighbors, coworkers, and eventually to the entire world. Thank you for giving me a taste of the kingdom while I'm here on earth. It helps me anticipate with joy the glory of heaven. I come to you in the name of Jesus, my Lord. Amen.

LENTEN ACTION

Do an anonymous act of kindness today for someone. It doesn't count if he or she catches you!

DAY 15

WEDNESDAY OF THE SECOND WEEK OF LENT

The Personal Freedom Required for Good Decisions

GO FOR THE GOAL!—WITH FREEDOM OF HEART

Therefore, we must make ourselves indifferent to all created things, as far as we are allowed free choice and are not under any prohibition. Consequently, as far as we are concerned, we should not prefer health to sickness, riches to poverty, honor to dishonor, a long life to a short life. The same holds for all other things.

SPIRITUAL EXERCISE, NO. 23
THE SPIRITUAL EXERCISES OF ST. IGNATIUS, 12

WHERE "TREASURE?" THERE HEART!

*"Do not store up for yourselves treasures on earth, where moth
and rust consume and where thieves break in and steal; but store
up for yourselves treasures in heaven, where neither moth nor
rust consumes and where thieves do not break in and steal. For
where your treasure is, there your heart will be also.*

*"No one can serve two masters; for a slave will either hate
the one and love the other, or be devoted to the one and despise
the other. You cannot serve God and wealth."*

MATTHEW 6:19–21, 24

PRAYER

Dear Lord, you know how much I long for praise, success,
possessions, and power. Yet, Saint Ignatius points out that in
order to be the person I am created to be, I must not prefer
these things over their opposite. The point is to want what
you, Lord, want, because *you* want it, the way *you* want it, for
as long as *you* want it. Help me to want to do *your* will. Amen.

LENTEN ACTION

Strive to live today free from all expectations, giving thanks
for each event and each person in your day. Look especially
for God's hand in those things you would normally not have
chosen.

DAY 16

The Origin of All Sins

INGRATITUDE

*I*t seems to me in the light of the Divine Goodness....that ingratitude is the most abominable of sins....For it is a forgetting of the graces, benefits, and blessings received. As such it is the cause, beginning, and origin of all sins and misfortunes. On the contrary, the grateful acknowledgment of blessings and gifts received is loved and esteemed not only on earth but in heaven.

LETTERS OF ST. IGNATIUS OF LOYOLA "TO SIMON RODRIQUES," 55

REBELLIOUS CHILDREN

> *The vision of Isaiah son of Amoz...*
> *Hear, O heavens, and listen, O earth;*
>   *for the Lord has spoken:*
> *I reared children and brought them up,*
>   *but they have rebelled against me.*

The ox knows its owner,
  and the donkey its master's crib;
but Israel does not know,
  my people do not understand.

Ah, sinful nation…
  who have despised the Holy One of Israel,
  who are utterly estranged!

I do not delight in the blood of bulls,
  or of lambs, or of goats.

Wash yourselves; make yourselves clean;
  remove the evil of your doings
  from before my eyes;
cease to do evil,
  learn to do good;
seek justice,
  rescue the oppressed,
defend the orphan,
  plead for the widow.

ISAIAH 1:1–4, 11, 16–17

PRAYER

Dear Lord, please help me to have a grateful heart. When I feel "entitled," it always leads me toward selfishness and eventually into sin. I want to follow you joyfully. I want my joy to be contagious to those I meet, so that together we may rejoice in your love. This I ask in your holy name. Amen.

LENTEN ACTION

Be conscious today of finding a reason to say "thank you" to family, friends, coworkers, and others that you meet. At the end of the day, make up your own Litany of Thanks and say it aloud.

DAY 17

FRIDAY OF THE SECOND WEEK OF LENT

The First Sin

FROM GRACE TO HATRED

*A*pply the memory to the sin of the angels, that is, recalling that they were created in the state of grace, that they did not want to make use of the freedom God gave them to reverence and obey their Creator and Lord, and so falling into pride, were changed from grace to hatred of God, and cast out of heaven into hell.

So, too, the understanding is to be used to think over the matter more in detail, and then the will to rouse more deeply the emotions.

SPIRITUAL EXERCISE, NO. 50
THE SPIRITUAL EXERCISES OF ST. IGNATIUS, 26–27

FROM ANGEL TO DEVIL

For if God did not spare the angels when they sinned, but cast them into hell and committed them to chains of deepest darkness to be kept until the judgement;...then the Lord knows how to rescue the godly from trial, and to keep the unrighteous under punishment until the day of judgement—especially those who indulge their flesh in depraved lust, and who despise authority....

2 PETER 2:4, 9–10

PRAYER

My Father in heaven, if the angels could fall, how can there any hope for me? I know that there would be no hope without your intervention and your love. I thank you for your love, and for Jesus, who came to show me how to be fully human. This prayer I make in the name of Christ our Lord, Amen.

LENTEN ACTION

Think about the sin of the angels—the sin of pride. What sins in your life are actually rooted in pride? Make an effort to do something contrary to what your pride tells you to do in a situation today.

DAY 18

SATURDAY OF THE SECOND WEEK OF LENT

The Second Sin

THE SIN OF OUR FIRST PARENTS

*R*ecall to mind the second sin, that of our First Parents. After Adam had been created on the Plain of Damascus and placed in the Garden of Paradise, and Eve had been formed from his side, they sinned by violating the command not to eat of the tree of knowledge. Thereafter, they were clothed in garments of skin and cast out of Paradise. By their sin they lost original justice, and for the rest of their lives, lived without it in many labors and great penance.

...[T]he understanding is to be used to think over the matter in greater detail, and the will ...as explained above.

SPIRITUAL EXERCISE, NO. 51
THE SPIRITUAL EXERCISES OF ST. IGNATIUS, 27

"YOU WILL BE LIKE GOD"

Now the serpent...said to the woman, "Did God say, 'You shall not eat from any tree in the garden'?" The woman said to the serpent, "We may eat of the fruit of the trees in the garden; but God said, 'You shall not eat of the fruit of the tree that is in the middle of the garden, nor shall you touch it, or you shall die.' " But the serpent said to the woman, "You will not die; for God knows that when you eat of it your eyes will be opened, and you will be like God, knowing good and evil."...[S]he took of its fruit and ate; and she also gave some to her husband...Then the eyes of both were opened, and they knew that they were naked;...

GENESIS 3:1–7

PRAYER

Lord, Eve circles around and around the tree after the serpent makes his suggestion—exposing herself to its attraction. Temptation always presents itself under the guise of something good! How often I am like Eve, exposing myself to "occasions of sin," thinking that I am smart enough, strong enough to resist. Pride is at the root. I want to decide for myself what is good and what is evil. Help me follow your way, for it leads to life! Amen.

LENTEN ACTION

What are the "occasions of sin" in your life? Jot them down and resolve to avoid them today.

DAY 19

The Third Sin

"ONE PERSON WHO WENT TO HELL"

*D*o the same with regard to the third sin, namely, that of one person who went to hell because of one mortal sin. Consider also countless others who have been lost for fewer sins than I have committed.

...Recall to memory the gravity and malice of sin against our Creator and Lord. Use the understanding to consider that because of sin, and of acting against Infinite Goodness, one is justly condemned forever. Close with the acts of the will....

SPIRITUAL EXERCISE, NO. 52
THE SPIRITUAL EXERCISES OF ST. IGNATIUS, 27–28

DIVES AND LAZARUS

"There was a rich man who was dressed in purple and fine linen and who feasted sumptuously every day. And at his gate lay a poor man named Lazarus, covered with sores, who longed to satisfy his hunger with what fell from the rich man's table....The poor man died and was carried away by the angels to be with Abraham. The rich man also died and was buried. In Hades, where he was being tormented, he looked up and saw Abraham far away with Lazarus by his side.... But Abraham said...'between you and us a great chasm has been fixed, so that those who might want to pass from here to you cannot do so, and no one can cross from there to us.' "

LUKE 16:19–21, 22–23, 25–26

PRAYER

Lord, as I read this Gospel, I realize that the rich man was not overtly cruel to Lazarus. He simply did not do anything to relieve his suffering. Please help me see not only my sins of commission, but those of omission. I long for a heart like yours—filled with love, truth, and compassion. Amen.

LENTEN ACTION

Examine the last week. Were there times that you could have acted in charity and compassion, but did nothing? Today, when the Holy Spirit inspires you to do something that is kind and generous, do it!

DAY 20

My Sin and Sinfulness

TEARS FOR MY SINS

I ask for what I desire. Here it will be to ask for a growing and intense sorrow and tears for my sins.

...I will call to mind all the sins of my life, reviewing year by year, and period by period.

I will consider who God is against whom I have sinned...His goodness with my wickedness.

I will conclude...extolling the mercy of God our Lord, pouring out my thoughts to Him, and giving thanks to Him that up to this very moment He has granted me life. I will resolve with His grace to amend for the future.

SPIRITUAL EXERCISES, NOS. 55, 56, 59, 61
THE SPIRITUAL EXERCISES OF ST. IGNATIUS, 29–30

"YOU ARE THE MAN!"

In the morning David wrote a letter to Joab....."Set Uriah in the forefront of the hardest fighting, and then draw back from him, so that he may be struck down and die."... [T]he Lord sent Nathan to David....."There were two men in a certain city, one rich and the other poor. The rich man had very many flocks and herds; but the poor man had nothing but one little ewe lamb....like a daughter to him. Now there came a traveller to the rich man, and...he took the poor man's lamb, and prepared that for the guest who had come to him." Then David's anger was greatly kindled against the man. He said to Nathan, "As the Lord lives, the man who has done this deserves to die....."

Nathan said to David, "You are the man!"

2 SAMUEL 11:14–15; 12:1–7

PRAYER

God my Father, I am so grateful that David, although he committed terrible sins, was still loved by you. Help me to have David's humility—to acknowledge my sins, to ask for forgiveness, and to try harder to live your commandments. Thank you for sending Jesus to show me the way. Amen.

LENTEN ACTION

Is there a sin that you consider the "worst" you have ever committed? Thinking of how much God loves you and wants you to be in communion with him, acknowledge your sin and ask God's help in overcoming the wounds this sin has caused.

DAY 21

Be Attentive: Review and Resolve

METHOD OF MAKING THE
GENERAL EXAMINATION OF CONSCIENCE

There are five points in this method.

1. ...[G]ive thanks to God our Lord for the favors received.

2. ...[A]sk for grace to know my sins and to rid myself of them.

3. ...[D]emand an account of my soul from the time of rising up to the present examination. I should go over one hour after another, one period after another. The thoughts should be examined first, then the words, and finally, the deeds in the same order as was explained under the Particular Examination of Conscience.

4. ...[A]sk pardon of God our Lord for my faults.

5. ...[R]esolve to amend with the grace of God.

SPIRITUAL EXERCISE, NO. 43
THE SPIRITUAL EXERCISES OF ST. IGNATIUS, 23

"IF OUR HEARTS DO NOT CONDEMN US"

Little children, let us love, not in word or speech, but in truth and action. Beloved, if our hearts do not condemn us, we have boldness before God; and we receive from him whatever we ask, because we obey his commandments and do what pleases him.

And this is his commandment, that we should believe in the name of his Son Jesus Christ and love one another, just as he has commanded us. All who obey his commandments abide in him, and he abides in them. And by this we know that he abides in us, by the Spirit that he has given us.

1 JOHN 3:18, 21–24

PRAYER

Dear Lord, the Church tells us that there are seven deep and pervasive temptations to sin—covetousness, lust, pride, anger, gluttony, envy and sloth. I want to identify the ways that they manifest themselves in my life. Help me to see my sinfulness, have sorrow for it, and root it out. This I ask in the name of Jesus the Lord. Amen.

LENTEN ACTION

Yesterday you identified your "worst" sin. Today, think of a virtue that would counteract it. Some possibilities include countering selfishness with generosity, pride with humility, and anger with gratitude. Concentrate now on living the virtue, not fighting the sin.

DAY 22

God Gazes Down Compassionately on Our Sinful World

I SEE THE THREE DIVINE PERSONS, THE EARTH IN BLINDNESS, AND OUR LADY

*T*his is to ask...for an intimate knowledge of our Lord, who has become man for me, that I may love Him more and follow Him more closely.

First, [see] those on the face of the earth....some at peace, and some at war; some weeping, some laughing;...

Secondly, I will see and consider the Three Divine Persons. They look down upon the whole surface of the earth, and behold all nations in great blindness, going down to death and descending into hell.

Thirdly, I will see our Lady and the angel saluting her.

I will reflect upon this to draw profit....

SPIRITUAL EXERCISES, NOS. 104, 106
THE SPIRITUAL EXERCISES OF ST. IGNATIUS, 49–50

The Lord Looked Down From His Holy Height

Let this be recorded for a generation to come,
so that a people yet unborn may praise the Lord:
that he looked down from his holy height,
from heaven the Lord looked at the earth,
to hear the groans of the prisoners,
to set free those who were doomed to die;
so that the name of the Lord may be declared in Zion,
and his praise in Jerusalem,
when peoples gather together,
and kingdoms, to worship the Lord.

PSALM 102:18–22

Prayer

God, if I had been in your position looking at the world with all of its sins and troubles, I doubt that my reaction would have been like yours. I cannot imagine that I would have looked on with such compassion and desire to set things right again. Thank you for your love, which is steadfast, generous, and always creative! It is only through your initiative that I am saved. In the name of Christ the Lord, Amen.

Lenten Action

Pretend you are God the Father looking down upon the world as you page slowly through today's newspaper. In some items you will rejoice. In others you will grieve. See if you are moved to take some action. If so, record that action in your journal.

DAY 23

THURSDAY OF THE THIRD WEEK OF LENT

God Deliberates, Discerns, and Decides

"I HEAR WHAT THE DIVINE PERSONS SAY..."

*T*hen I will listen to what the persons on the face of the earth say, that is, how they speak to one another, swear and blaspheme, etc. I will also hear what the Divine Persons say, that is, "Let us work the redemption of the human race," etc. Then I will listen to what the angel and our Lady say. Finally, I will reflect upon all I hear to draw profit from their words.

...[T]he Divine Persons do...work the most holy Incarnation.... [O]ur Lady humbles herself, and offers thanks to the Divine Majesty.

SPIRITUAL EXERCISES, NOS. 107, 108
THE SPIRITUAL EXERCISES OF ST. IGNATIUS, 50–51

THE LIGHT SHINES IN THE DARKNESS

In the beginning was the Word, and the Word was with God, and the Word was God. He was in the beginning with God. All things came into being through him, and without him not one thing came into being. What has come into being in him was life, and the life was the light of all people. The light shines in the darkness, and the darkness did not overcome it.

JOHN 1:1–5

PRAYER

Oh my God, what a miracle! That you would love us enough to become one of us! How astounding your love is. How far beyond our ways are your ways! Thank you for being the light in our darkness. And Mary, thank you for saying "yes" to God, even when you did not understand everything that was being asked of you. I offer this prayer in Jesus' name. Amen.

LENTEN ACTION

Imagine that you are with the Trinity at the moment that they decide how to redeem the human race. Then, imagine Mary not only saying "yes," but giving thanks for the opportunity to bear the Son of God!

DAY 24

FRIDAY OF THE THIRD WEEK OF LENT

Coming to Know and Follow Jesus

THE ANNUNCIATION TO OUR LADY

*T*he angel, St. Gabriel, salutes our Lady, and announces to her the conception of Christ our Lord....

The angel confirms what he had said to her by announcing to her the conception of St. John the Baptist....

Our Lady replied to the angel....

SPIRITUAL EXERCISE, NO. 262
THE SPIRITUAL EXERCISES OF ST. IGNATIUS, 115

"Let it Be With Me According to Your Word"

In the sixth month the angel Gabriel was sent by God to a town in Galilee called Nazareth, to a virgin engaged to a man whose name was Joseph, of the house of David. The virgin's name was Mary. And he came to her and said, "Greetings, favoured one! The Lord is with you." But she was much perplexed by his words and pondered what sort of greeting this might be. The angel said to her, "Do not be afraid, Mary, for you have found favour with God. And now, you will conceive in your womb and bear a son, and you will name him Jesus. He will be great, and will be called the Son of the Most High....of his kingdom there will be no end." Then Mary said, "Here am I, the servant of the Lord; let it be with me according to your word."...

LUKE 1:26–33, 38

Prayer

Jesus, I am amazed by your mother's maturity and humility. I would have had a thousand questions: Why me? What then? What will people say? What will happen? But Mary's eyes were clearer than mine. She knew that if God wanted this, she wanted to cooperate in his plan. Help me to have a docile heart and a discerning spirit like Mary. This I ask in your holy name, Amen.

Lenten Action

Try to recall an occasion when you have been shocked and confused by a prompting to do something you didn't expect. How did you decide whether it was an invitation from God or an enticement from an evil spirit? Try to identify with Mary in this story.

DAY 25

Beginning of the Public Life of Jesus

"SEE IN IMAGINATION...
WHERE CHRIST OUR LORD PREACHED"

*I*n the preparatory prayer I will beg God our Lord for grace that all my intentions, actions, and operations may be directed purely to the praise and service of His Divine Majesty.

SPIRITUAL EXERCISE, NO. 46
THE SPIRITUAL EXERCISES OF ST. IGNATIUS, 25

First Prelude. This is a mental representation of the place. Here it will be to see in imagination the synagogues, villages, and towns where Christ our Lord preached.

Second Prelude. I will ask for the grace I desire. Here it will be to ask of our Lord the grace not to be deaf to his call, but prompt and diligent to accomplish His most holy will.

SPIRITUAL EXERCISE, NO. 91
THE SPIRITUAL EXERCISES OF ST. IGNATIUS, 43

"TODAY THIS SCRIPTURE HAS BEEN FULFILLED IN YOUR HEARING"

When he came to Nazareth, where he had been brought up, he went to the synagogue on the sabbath day, as was his custom. He stood up to read, and the scroll of the prophet Isaiah was given to him. He unrolled the scroll and found the place where it was written:

"The Spirit of the Lord is upon me,
 because he has anointed me
 to bring good news to the poor.
He has sent me to proclaim release to the captives
 and recovery of sight to the blind,
 to let the oppressed go free,
to proclaim the year of the Lord's favour."
And he rolled up the scroll, gave it back to the attendant, and sat down. The eyes of all in the synagogue were fixed on him. Then he began to say to them, "Today this scripture has been fulfilled in your hearing."

LUKE 4:16–21

PRAYER

Lord, I live more than two thousand years after your birth. Long before I was born, my ancestors and their neighbors knew you. The country in which I live is built on many of the principles of Christianity. In a way, I have always known you. Yet, do I know you—or just know about you? Inspired by the example of Saint Ignatius, I want to know you, love you, and follow you all the days of my life. Amen.

LENTEN ACTION

Imagine that you are in the synagogue with Jesus when he reads the passage from Isaiah and announces that it is being fulfilled before your eyes. How do you feel? What do you think? Talk with Jesus about your desire to follow him.

DAY 26

THE FOURTH SUNDAY OF LENT

Imagine the Call of a Generous Earthly King

THE CALL OF AN EARTHLY KING

[P]lace before my mind a human king, chosen by God...to whom all Christian...people pay homage....

[C]onsider the address this king makes to all his subjects...: "It is my will to conquer all the lands of the infidel. Therefore, whoever wishes to join with me...must be content with the same food, drink, clothing, etc. as mine....[H]e must work with me by day, and watch with me by night, etc., that as he has had a share in the toil with me, afterwards, he may share in the victory with me."

[C]onsider what the answer of good subjects ought to be to a king so generous....[I]f anyone would refuse the invitation of such a king, how justly he would deserve to be condemned by the whole world....

SPIRITUAL EXERCISES, NOS. 92–94
THE SPIRITUAL EXERCISES OF ST. IGNATIUS, 43–44

"THE LORD SAID TO YOU: 'IT IS YOU WHO SHALL BE SHEPHERD OF MY PEOPLE'"

Then all the tribes of Israel came to David at Hebron, and said, "Look, we are your bone and flesh. For some time, while Saul was king over us, it was you who led out Israel and brought it in. The Lord said to you: It is you who shall be shepherd of my people Israel, you who shall be ruler over Israel." So all the elders of Israel came to the king at Hebron; and King David made a covenant with them at Hebron before the Lord, and they anointed David king over Israel. David was thirty years old when he began to reign, and he reigned for forty years. At Hebron he reigned over Judah for seven years and six months; and at Jerusalem he reigned over all Israel and Judah for thirty-three years.

2 SAMUEL 5:1–5

PRAYER

Lord, with your grace, may my heart awaken to loyalty and devotion only to a leader whose cause is worthy and who is a genuine companion with those he or she leads—a leader like Jesus, in whose name we offer this prayer. Amen.

LENTEN ACTION

Think of a person whom you have admired and on whom you have modeled your outlook and behavior—maybe when you were an adolescent or a young adult. What attracted you to that person? List the qualities.

DAY 27

MONDAY OF THE FOURTH WEEK OF LENT

The Call of Christ, the Eternal King

"FOLLOW ME IN GLORY"

Christ our Lord, the Eternal King...addresses the words: "It is my will to conquer the whole world and all my enemies ... [W]hoever wishes to join me in this enterprise must be willing to labor with me, that by following me in suffering, he may follow me in glory."

... [A]ll persons who have judgment and reason will offer themselves entirely for this work.

...Those who wish to give greater proof of their love...will not only offer themselves entirely for the work, but will act against their sensuality and carnal and worldly love, and make offerings of greater value....

SPIRITUAL EXERCISES, NOS. 95–97
THE SPIRITUAL EXERCISES OF ST. IGNATIUS, 44–45

"MY KINGDOM IS NOT FROM THIS WORLD"

Then Pilate entered the headquarters again, summoned Jesus, and asked him, "Are you the King of the Jews?" Jesus answered, "My kingdom is not from this world. If my kingdom were from this world, my followers would be fighting to keep me from being handed over to the Jews. But as it is, my kingdom is not from here." Pilate asked him, "So you are a king?" Jesus answered, "You say that I am a king. For this I was born, and for this I came into the world, to testify to the truth. Everyone who belongs to the truth listens to my voice." Pilate asked him, "What is truth?"

JOHN 18:33, 36–38

PRAYER

Lord, help me to hear your call to join you in overcoming the powers of evil. Enable me to work with you to establish the kingdom of God—in my family, my work, my neighborhood—reaching socially beyond to bring peace and justice throughout this world. This we ask in the name of Christ the Lord, Amen.

LENTEN ACTION

List the characteristics Jesus had that made people want to follow him. Do you have any of those characteristics? Ask the Lord if there are concrete steps you need to take to develop as a Christ-like leader.

DAY 28

The Full and Generous Offering of Oneself to Christ the King

IGNATIUS' PRAYER OF FULL DEDICATION

*E*ternal Lord of all things, in the presence of Thy infinite good-ness, and of Thy glorious mother, and of all the saints of Thy heavenly court, this is the offering of myself which I make with Thy favor and help. I protest that it is my earnest desire and my deliber-ate choice, provided only it is for Thy greater service and praise, to imitate Thee in bearing all wrongs and all abuse and all poverty, both actual and spiritual, should Thy most holy majesty deign to choose and admit me to such a state and way of life.

SPIRITUAL EXERCISE, NO. 98
THE SPIRITUAL EXERCISES OF ST. IGNATIUS, 45

"YOU KNOW THAT I LOVE YOU"

When they had finished breakfast, Jesus said to Simon Peter, "Simon son of John, do you love me more than these?" He said to him, "Yes, Lord; you know that I love you." Jesus said to him, "Feed my lambs." A second time he said to him, "Simon son of John, do you love me?" He said to him, "Yes, Lord; you know that I love you." Jesus said to him, "Tend my sheep." He said to him the third time, "Simon son of John, do you love me?" Peter felt hurt because he said to him the third time, "Do you love me?" And he said to him, "Lord, you know everything; you know that I love you." Jesus said to him, "Feed my sheep."... After this he said to him, "Follow me."

JOHN 21:15–17, 19

PRAYER

Lord, under the inspiration of Saint Ignatius, I offer myself to you. "I protest that it is my earnest desire and my deliberate choice, provided only it is for Thy greater service and praise, to imitate Thee in bearing all wrongs and all abuse" in the work of spreading your kingdom of love and peace in the world. Amen.

LENTEN ACTION

In your service of the Lord have you already experienced "wrongs and abuse" at the hands of another? If your paths still cross, are you willing to engage that other person in conversation and reconciliation? Discern whether and how God might be asking you to do so.

DAY 29

The Two Fundamental Options in Life

TWO STANDARDS OR BANNERS
UNDER WHICH WE CAN SERVE

*T*he one of Christ, our supreme leader and lord, and the other of Lucifer, the deadly enemy of our human nature.

The First Prelude....Christ calls and wants all beneath His standard, and Lucifer, on the other hand, wants all under his.

The Second Prelude....[S]ee a great plain, comprising the whole region about Jerusalem, where the sovereign Commander-in-Chief of all the good is Christ our Lord; and another plain about the region of Babylon, where the chief of the enemy is Lucifer.

The Third Prelude....[A]sk for a knowledge of the deceits of the rebel chief and help to guard myself against them; and also to ask for knowledge of the true life exemplified in the sovereign and true Commander, and the grace to imitate Him.

SPIRITUAL EXERCISES NOS. 136–139
THE SPIRITUAL EXERCISES OF ST. IGNATIUS, 60

"I HAVE SET BEFORE YOU LIFE AND DEATH, BLESSINGS AND CURSES"

See, I have set before you today life and prosperity, death and adversity. If you obey the commandments of the Lord your God that I am commanding you today, by loving the Lord your God, walking in his ways, and observing his commandments, decrees, and ordinances, then you shall live and become numerous, and the Lord your God will bless you in the land that you are entering to possess. I call heaven and earth to witness against you today that I have set before you life and death, blessings and curses. Choose life so that you and your descendants may live, loving the Lord your God, obeying him, and holding fast to him; for that means life to you and length of days....

DEUTERONOMY 30:15–16, 19–20

PRAYER

Lord, help me to realize and appreciate that there are indeed two totally different life options: self-promotion or loving service of others. Please support my choice of a loving life of service in companionship with you, now and forever. Amen.

LENTEN ACTION

Seven or eight times today, say, "Lord, that I might see!"— with Bartimaeus, the blind beggar beside the road leading out of Jericho.

DAY 30

Satan's Malignant Intent

COVET RICHES→EMPTY HONORS→OVERWEENING PRIDE→ALL OTHER VICES

*I*magine you see the chief of all the enemy…seated on a great throne of fire and smoke, his appearance inspiring horror and terror.

Consider how he summons innumerable demons, and scatters them…throughout the whole world.…

Consider the address he makes to them, how he goads them on to lay snares for men.…First they are to tempt them to covet riches… that they may the more easily attain the empty honors of this world, and then come to overweening pride.

…From these three steps the evil one leads to all other vices.

SPIRITUAL EXERCISES, NOS. 140–142
THE SPIRITUAL EXERCISES OF ST. IGNATIUS, 60–61

The Works of the "Flesh"

Live by the Spirit, I say, and do not gratify the desires of the flesh. For what the flesh desires is opposed to the Spirit, and what the Spirit desires is opposed to the flesh; for these are opposed to each other, to prevent you from doing what you want.… Now the works of the flesh are obvious: fornication, impurity, licentiousness, idolatry, sorcery, enmities, strife, jealousy, anger, quarrels, dissensions, factions, envy, drunkenness, carousing, and things like these. I am warning you, as I warned you before: those who do such things will not inherit the kingdom of God.

GALATIANS 5:16–21

Prayer

Lord, please help me to believe in a living power of evil in this world. Give me the grace of horror for such a malignant intent to destroy us humans by inciting each of us to exploit all others for the sake of self-promotion and by corrupting our culture to convince us that this is the enlightened way to live. Amen.

Lenten Action

Compare the causes of our recent economic meltdown to Satan's strategy to tempt us to riches, then honors, and then pride. See a connection?

DAY 31

Grounded in Christ

WILLINGNESS AND DESIRE FOR POVERTY→
INSULTS→HUMILITY →ALL OTHER VIRTUES

*C*onsider Christ our Lord, standing in a lowly place in a great plain about the region of Jerusalem....

Consider how the Lord...chooses so many persons...and sends them throughout the whole world....

Consider the address which Christ our Lord makes ...[H]elp all, first by attracting them to the highest spiritual poverty, and should it please the Divine Majesty...even to actual poverty. Secondly,...a desire for insults and contempt, for from these springs humility.

Hence, there will be three steps: the first, poverty as opposed to riches; the second, insults or contempt as opposed to the honor of this world; the third, humility as opposed to pride. From these three steps, let them lead [people] to all other virtues.

SPIRITUAL EXERCISES, NOS. 143–146
THE SPIRITUAL EXERCISES OF ST. IGNATIUS, 61–62

THE FRUIT OF THE SPIRIT

[T]he fruit of the Spirit is love, joy, peace, patience, kindness, generosity, faithfulness, gentleness, and self-control. There is no law against such things. And those who belong to Christ Jesus have crucified the flesh with its passions and desires. If we live by the Spirit, let us also be guided by the Spirit. Let us not become conceited, competing against one another, envying one another.

GALATIANS 5:22–26

PRAYER

Lord, please give me such confidence in your love, appreciation, and joyful affirmation of me that I can bear peacefully the insults of others. Keep reminding me that humility means "to be grounded," and that when I am grounded, in you I bring forth the fruits of the Holy Spirit. Amen.

LENTEN ACTION

Do a short Examination of Conscience on whether you habitually keep possessions, prestige, and personal pride in their proper "second place" as means to your love of God and others. It might help to go back and read Day 21 on the Examination.

DAY 32

Embodied in Action

WHAT THE WORLD AND CHRIST LOVE AND EMBRACE

*I*t helps and profits in the spiritual life to abhor in its totality and not in part whatever the world loves and embraces, and to accept and desire with all possible energy whatever Christ our Lord has loved and embraced. Just as the men of the world who follow the world love and seek with such great diligence honors, fame, and esteem for a great name on earth, as the world teaches them, so those who proceed spiritually and truly follow Christ our Lord love and intensely desire everything opposite.

THE CONSTITUTIONS OF THE SOCIETY OF JESUS
AND THEIR COMPLEMENTARY NORMS

THE PHARISEE AND THE PUBLICAN

He also told this parable to some who trusted in themselves that they were righteous and regarded others with contempt: "Two men went up to the temple to pray, one a Pharisee and the other a tax-collector. The Pharisee, standing by himself, was praying thus, 'God, I thank you that I am not like other people: thieves, rogues, adulterers, or even like this tax-collector. I fast twice a week; I give a tenth of all my income.' But the tax-collector, standing far off, would not even look up to heaven, but was beating his breast and saying, 'God, be merciful to me, a sinner!' I tell you, this man went down to his home justified rather than the other; for all who exalt themselves will be humbled, but all who humble themselves will be exalted.'"

LUKE 18:9–14

PRAYER

Lord, help me always to beg confidently for your forgiveness like the tax collector and never boastfully like the Pharisee so that I may grow daily in the likeness of Jesus, with and through whom I offer this prayer. Amen.

LENTEN ACTION

Try to think of two people you've known, one of whom resembles the tax collector, the other of whom resembles the Pharisee. Jot in your journal what you've learned from each.

DAY 33

THE FIFTH SUNDAY OF LENT

The Strategy of Satan

ATTACK AT THE WEAKEST POINT

*T*he conduct of our enemy may also be compared to the tactics of a leader intent upon seizing and plundering a position he desires. A commander and leader of an army will encamp, explore the fortifications and defenses of the stronghold, and attack at the weakest point. In the same way, the enemy of our human nature investigates from every side....Where he finds the defenses of eternal salvation weakest and most deficient, there he attacks and tries to take us by storm.

SPIRITUAL EXERCISE, NO. 327
THE SPIRITUAL EXERCISES OF ST. IGNATIUS, 146

THE HUMILIATION OF SELF-EXALTATION

Then Jesus said to the crowds and to his disciples, "The scribes and the Pharisees sit on Moses' seat; therefore, do whatever they teach you and follow it; but do not do as they do, for they do not practise what they teach. They tie up heavy burdens, hard to bear, and lay them on the shoulders of others; but they themselves are unwilling to lift a finger to move them. They do all their deeds to be seen by others....All who exalt themselves will be humbled, and all who humble themselves will be exalted."

MATTHEW 23:1–12

PRAYER

Lord, give me the wisdom to recognize where and how I am vulnerable to Satan's effort to bring me low. Help me to join you in your humble service of others, and thereby to join you in the peaceful self-confidence that the world cannot give. Amen.

LENTEN ACTION

Try to diagnose where you are most vulnerable to Satan's attack or wiles. Verify your diagnosis with a good friend and confidant.

DAY 34

Jesus Faces Rejection and Death

A PRAYER FOR AFFRONTS

*M*ay it please the Mother of God to hear my prayer for you, which is that you may meet with even greater affronts so that you may have the occasion of greater merit, provided that you can accept them with patience and constancy and without sin on the part of others, remembering the greater insults which Christ our Lord suffered for us.

LETTERS OF ST. IGNATIUS OF LOYOLA
"TO ISABEL ROSER," 11

JESUS' FIRST SERMON IN NAZARETH

And [Jesus] said, "Truly I tell you, no prophet is accepted in the prophet's home town. But the truth is, there were many widows in Israel in the time of Elijah, when the heaven was shut up for three years and six months, and there was a severe famine over all the land; yet Elijah was sent to none of them except to a widow at Zarephath in Sidon...." When they heard this, all in the synagogue were filled with rage. They got up, drove him out of the town, and led him to the brow of the hill on which their town was built, so that they might hurl him off the cliff. But he passed through the midst of them and went on his way.

LUKE 4:24–30

PRAYER

Lord, I sympathize with you in your experience of rejection for sharing God's wisdom with others. Strengthen my fidelity and commitment to the truth of God's wisdom, cost what it might. Amen.

LENTEN ACTION

Jesus' rejection was the more painful in that it came from former friends and close neighbors. Have you experienced misunderstanding and rejection from friends and neighbors, or even family? How have you continued to relate to them in a Christ-like way? Record your efforts in your journal for future reference.

DAY 35

Struggles With Pharisees and Scribes

SERVICE OF GOD INFURIATES "THE WORLD"

*Y*ou speak of the enmities, the intrigues, and the untruths which have been circulated about you. 1 am not at all surprised at this, not even if it were worse than it is. For just as soon as you determined to bend every effort to secure the praise, honor, and service of God our Lord, you declared war against the world and raised your standard in its face, and got ready to reject what is lofty by embracing what is lowly....

LETTERS OF ST. IGNATIUS OF LOYOLA
"TO ISABEL ROSER," 11

A Sabbath Miracle Invites Persecution

After this there was a festival of the Jews, and Jesus went up to Jerusalem.

Now in Jerusalem by the Sheep Gate there is a pool, called in Hebrew Beth-zatha, which has five porticoes. In these lay many invalids—blind, lame, and paralysed. One man was there who had been ill for thirty-eight years. When Jesus saw him lying there and knew that he had been there a long time, he said to him..."Stand up, take your mat and walk." At once the man was made well, and he took up his mat and began to walk.

Now that day was a sabbath. The man went away and told the Jews that it was Jesus who had made him well. Therefore the Jews started persecuting Jesus, because he was doing such things on the sabbath.

JOHN 5:1–6, 8–9, 15–16

Prayer

Lord, my desire to be respected and affirmed by others threatens occasionally to become the primary motive for my good deeds. As an antidote to this temptation, please give me the courage to risk ridicule for good deeds on other occasions. Amen.

Lenten Action

Do you have relatives or friends who scoff at religion? If an occasion offers, tell one of them casually how much you enjoy praying through Lent with this book. See if their reaction opens a door for profitable conversation.

DAY 36

WEDNESDAY OF THE FIFTH WEEK OF LENT

They Picked Up Stones to Throw at Him

SEEKING THE TRUTH LOVINGLY

To assure better cooperation between the one who is giving the Exercises and the exercitant, and more beneficial results for both, it is necessary to suppose that every good Christian is more ready to put a good interpretation on another's statement than to condemn it as false. If an orthodox construction cannot be put on a proposition, the one who made it should be asked how he understands it. If he is in error, he should be corrected with all kindness. If this does not suffice, all appropriate means should be used to bring him to a correct interpretation, and so defend the proposition from error.

SPIRITUAL EXERCISE, NO. 22
THE SPIRITUAL EXERCISES OF ST. IGNATIUS, 11

TAKING OFFENSE DEFENSIVELY

"Very truly, I tell you, whoever keeps my word will never see death." The Jews said to him, "Now we know that you have a demon. Abraham died, and so did the prophets; yet you say, 'Whoever keeps my word will never taste death.' Are you greater than our father Abraham, who died? The prophets also died...."

"Your ancestor Abraham rejoiced that he would see my day; he saw it and was glad." Then the Jews said to him, "You are not yet fifty years old, and have you seen Abraham?" Jesus said to them, "Very truly, I tell you, before Abraham was, I am." So they picked up stones to throw at him, but Jesus hid himself and went out of the temple.

JOHN 8:51–53, 56–59

PRAYER

Lord, help me to listen attentively to what people say and to especially try to understand what it means. Keep me open to learning new things and even to being challenged to stretch and grow in my outlook and attitude. Guide me along the continuing conversion of mind and heart that living your life demands. Amen.

LENTEN ACTION

Think of instances in your life when a mental "light" suddenly went on and you saw what something really meant for the first time. Eureka! Or think of how your attitude changed, either quickly or over time, about something you had regarded as wrong or silly and now recognize as helpful and right. Record these instances of insight and conversion for future reference.

DAY 37

Self-promotion or Self-giving?

REMEMBERING THE GREATER INSULTS
WHICH CHRIST SUFFERED FOR US

*J*f we wish absolutely to live in honor and to be held in esteem
by our neighbors, we can never be solidly rooted in God our
Lord, and it will be impossible for us to remain unscathed when we
meet with affronts....

LETTERS OF ST. IGNATIUS OF LOYOLA
"TO ISABEL ROSER," 11

"WE KNOW WHERE THIS MAN IS FROM"

...Jesus went up into the temple and began to teach. Now some of the people of Jerusalem were saying..."[W]e know where this man is from; but when the Messiah comes, no one will know where he is from." Then Jesus cried out..."I have not come on my own. But the one who sent me is true, and you do not know him. I know him, because I am from him, and he sent me." Then they tried to arrest him, but no one laid hands on him, because his hour had not yet come....[T]he chief priests and Pharisees sent temple police to arrest him.

JOHN 7:14, 25, 27–30, 32

PRAYER

Lord, help me to be like you in caring deeply and warmly about people and their goodness, but not needing their appreciation and approval for our own sense of worth. Grant me unshakable faith in your total and eternal affirmation so that I need live only in your eyes, and not in the eyes of others. Amen.

LENTEN ACTION

When we are not peacefully grounded in God's love, our reaction to real or imagined insults is either "fight" (pugnacious retaliation) or "flight" (escape or evasion). Think about which reaction you prefer.

DAY 38

Satan's "Gift" of Deceptive Happiness

GOD'S JOY AND SATAN'S MANIPULATION

*I*t is characteristic of God and His Angels, when they act upon the soul, to give true happiness and spiritual joy, and to banish all the sadness and disturbances which are caused by the enemy. It is characteristic of the evil one to fight against such happiness and consolation by proposing fallacious reasonings, subtleties, and continual deceptions.

SPIRITUAL EXERCISE, NO. 329

THE SPIRITUAL EXERCISES OF ST. IGNATIUS, 147

"LET US...GET HIS INHERITANCE"

"There was a landowner who planted a vineyard, put a fence around it, dug a wine press in it, and built a watch-tower. Then he leased it to tenants and went to another country. When the harvest time had come, he sent his slaves to the tenants to collect his produce. But the tenants seized his slaves and beat one, killed another, and stoned another. Again he sent other slaves, more than the first; and they treated them in the same way. Finally he sent his son to them, saying, 'They will respect my son.' But when the tenants saw the son, they said to themselves, 'This is the heir; come, let us kill him and get his inheritance.' So they seized him, threw him out of the vineyard, and killed him....."

When the chief priests and the Pharisees heard his parables, they realized that he was speaking about them. They wanted to arrest him, but they feared the crowds, because they regarded him as a prophet.

MATTHEW 21:33–39, 45–46

PRAYER

Lord, keep me constantly aware that my life, my family, all my human brothers and sisters, the property I hold, and the future I pursue are all your gifts to me, for which I have stewardship, not title. And let me thereby enjoy the deep consolation of perpetual gratitude to you, our Lord and Savior. Amen.

LENTEN ACTION

Pray Psalm 8 several times today. Key sentences are: "When I look at your heavens, what are humans that you are mindful of them? Yet you have given them dominion over the works of your hands. O Lord, how majestic is your name in all the earth!"

DAY 39

Only That the Truth May Appear

IGNATIUS INSISTS ON A TRIAL

*J*ust as he was about to leave [Paris], the pilgrim heard that an accusation had been lodged against him with the Inquisitor, and a process begun....The Inquisitor said that it was true there had been an accusation, but that he did not see that there was anything of importance in it. He only wanted to see what [Ignatius] had written in the Exercises....Nevertheless the pilgrim insisted that his case be brought to trial and that a sentence be passed. But, as the Inquisitor seemed unwilling to do this, the pilgrim brought a public notary and witnesses to the Inquisitor's house and received formal testimony of the whole affair.

ST. IGNATIUS' OWN STORY, 59–60

FOR WHICH GOOD WORK DO YOU STONE ME?

The Jews took up stones again to stone him. Jesus replied, "I have shown you many good works from the Father. For which of these are you going to stone me?" The Jews answered, "It is not for a good work that we are going to stone you, but for blasphemy, because you, though only a human being, are making yourself God."

"If I am not doing the works of my Father, then do not believe me. But if I do them, even though you do not believe me, believe the works, so that you may know and understand that the Father is in me and I am in the Father." Then they tried to arrest him again, but he escaped from their hands.

JOHN 10:31–33, 37–39

PRAYER

Lord, guide me through life on the sure and solid stepping stones of your truth so that I may never go astray through the connivance of people who are deceived by Satan. May your Holy Spirit be my counselor and advocate in all times and places. Amen.

LENTEN ACTION

Have you ever seriously misjudged someone—either their behavior or their intentions? When—and why—did you realize it was a MIS-judgment? What lesson(s) did you learn?

DAY 40

PALM SUNDAY

Royal Entry Into Jerusalem

SEEING, HEARING, AND RESPONDING
TO CHRIST OUR KING

THE KINGDOM OF CHRIST

The First Prelude. This is a mental representation of the place. Here it will be to see in imagination the synagogues, villages, and towns where Christ our Lord preached.

The Second Prelude. I will ask for the grace I desire. Here it will be to ask of our Lord the grace not to be deaf to His call, but prompt and diligent to accomplish His most holy will.

SPIRITUAL EXERCISE, NO. 91
THE SPIRITUAL EXERCISES OF ST. IGNATIUS, 43

SPREADING THEIR CLOAKS ON THE ROAD

[Jesus] sent two of the disciples, saying, "Go into the village ahead of you, and as you enter it you will find tied there a colt that has never been ridden. Untie it and bring it here."...As they were untying the colt, its owners asked them, "Why are you untying the colt?" They said, "The Lord needs it." Then they brought it to Jesus; and after throwing their cloaks on the colt, they set Jesus on it. As he rode along, people kept spreading their cloaks on the road.... [T]he whole multitude of the disciples began to praise God joyfully with a loud voice for all the deeds of power that they had seen, saying,
"Blessed is the king
   who comes in the name of the Lord!
Peace in heaven,
   and glory in the highest heaven!"

LUKE 19:29–39

PRAYER

Lord, I praise you joyfully with a loud voice for all the deeds of power that I have seen, saying, "Blessed is the king who comes in the name of the Lord! Peace in heaven, and glory in the highest heaven!" Now and forever. Amen

LENTEN ACTION

Ignatius' first introductory step ("prelude") in this meditation is to "see in imagination the synagogues, villages, and towns where Christ our Lord preached." Several times today, take a second or two to imagine Jesus riding down that hill to Jerusalem amid shouts of joy, knowing full well that it is to his death he goes.

DAY 41

Final Meal With Lazarus, Martha, and Mary

RULES FOR THE DISCERNMENT OF SPIRITS

*R*ules for understanding to some extent the different movements produced in the soul and for recognizing those that are good to admit them, and those that are bad, to reject them....

In the case of those who go from one mortal sin to another, the enemy is ordinarily accustomed to propose apparent pleasures.... the more readily to keep them in their vices and increase the number of their sins.

With such persons the good spirit uses a method which is the reverse of the above. Making use of the light of reason, he will rouse the sting of conscience and fill them with remorse.

SPIRITUAL EXERCISES, NOS. 313–314
THE SPIRITUAL EXERCISES OF ST. IGNATIUS, 141

MOTIVATIONS/MOVEMENTS: MARY AND JUDAS

Six days before the Passover Jesus came to Bethany, the home of Lazarus, whom he had raised from the dead. There they gave a dinner for him. Martha served....Mary took a pound of costly perfume made of pure nard, anointed Jesus' feet....But Judas Iscariot, one of his disciples (the one who was about to betray him), said, "Why was this perfume not sold for three hundred denarii and the money given to the poor?" ...Jesus said, "Leave her alone. She bought it so that she might keep it for the day of my burial."

When the great crowd of the Jews learned that he was there, they came not only because of Jesus but also to see Lazarus, whom he had raised from the dead. So the chief priests planned to put Lazarus to death as well....

JOHN 12:1–9

PRAYER

Lord, as Mary anointed your feet at this supper and as you washed your apostles' feet at the Last Supper, help me to regard all other people with the kind of reverence and care you asked of us when you said, "Do this in memory of me." Amen.

LENTEN ACTION

When Judas complained about Mary, Jesus spoke right up. "Leave her alone," he said to Judas. Can you speak your mind firmly, but kindly? Or does it come out angrily? Listen to yourself today. (Note: Doing this will be an exercise of "discernment of spirits!")

DAY 42

TUESDAY OF HOLY WEEK

Discerning Spirits

FEELING BAD ABOUT DOING GOOD—SATAN'S PLOY

*I*n the case of those who go on earnestly striving to cleanse their souls from sin and who seek to rise in the service of God our Lord to greater perfection, the method pursued is the opposite of that mentioned in the first rule [on Day 41].

Then it is characteristic of the evil spirit to harass with anxiety, to afflict with sadness, to raise obstacles backed by fallacious reasonings that disturb the soul. Thus he seeks to prevent the soul from advancing.

It is characteristic of the good spirit, however, to give courage and strength, consolations, tears, inspirations, and peace.

SPIRITUAL EXERCISE, NO. 315
THE SPIRITUAL EXERCISES OF ST. IGNATIUS, 141–142

FEELING GOOD ABOUT DOING GOOD—GOD'S WAY

When he had gone out, Jesus said, "Now the Son of Man has been glorified, and God has been glorified in him. If God has been glorified in him, God will also glorify him in himself and will glorify him at once. Little children, I am with you only a little longer. You will look for me; and as I said to the Jews so now I say to you, 'Where I am going, you cannot come.'"

Simon Peter said to him, "Lord, where are you going?" Jesus answered, "Where I am going, you cannot follow me now; but you will follow afterwards."

JOHN 13:31–33, 36

PRAYER

Lord, please give me during this Holy Week the mind of Peter, who felt distress that Jesus "was going away" on a journey on which Peter could not accompany him right now. Help me to feel a certain dread and fear of loss so that when your journey is completed on Easter, I may fully rejoice with you, now and forever. Amen.

LENTEN ACTION

List instances in your life when feeling really good was actually a desolation, because it was coaxing you into trouble. And then, if you have time, list a few instances in which feeling bad or uncomfortable (like Peter's dread) was really a consolation—a gift of God—because it led to something really constructive.

DAY 43

WEDNESDAY OF HOLY WEEK

The Betrayal

DESOLATION AND WHERE,
BY NATURE, IT TENDS TO LEAD US

I call desolation…darkness of soul, turmoil of spirit, inclination to what is low and earthly, restlessness rising from many disturbances and temptations which lead to want of faith, want of hope, want of love. The soul is wholly slothful, tepid, sad, and separated, as it were, from its Creator and Lord. For just as consolation is the opposite of desolation, so the thoughts that spring from consolation are the opposite of those that spring from desolation.

SPIRITUAL EXERCISE, NO. 317
THE SPIRITUAL EXERCISES OF ST. IGNATIUS, 142

WOE TO THAT ONE …

Then one of the twelve, who was called Judas Iscariot, went to the chief priests and said, "What will you give me if I betray him to you?" They paid him thirty pieces of silver. And from that moment he began to look for an opportunity to betray him.

On the first day of Unleavened Bread…[Jesus] took his place with the twelve; and while they were eating, he said, "Truly I tell you, one of you will betray me." And they became greatly distressed and began to say to him one after another, "Surely not I, Lord?" He answered, "The one who has dipped his hand into the bowl with me will betray me. The Son of Man goes as it is written of him, but woe to that one by whom the Son of Man is betrayed! It would have been better for that one not to have been born."

MATTHEW 26:14–17, 20–24

PRAYER

Lord, let me not be led into temptation by the manipulation of my feelings by Satan. Keep me alert and attentive so I can correctly discern my feelings and choose your will for myself wisely. May Christ be a model. Amen.

LENTEN ACTION

Try to think of an occasion in your life when desolation, because of the way you handled it, became a springboard rather than an impediment for you to do something helpful for other people out of concern for them. Maybe your very mood of sadness triggered compassion for their sad plight. Record it in your journal for future reference.

DAY 44

<small>HOLY THURSDAY</small>

The Servant Leader

CONSOLATION AND WHERE, BY NATURE, IT TENDS TO LEAD US

I call it consolation when an interior movement is aroused in the soul, by which it is inflamed with love of its Creator and Lord, and as a consequence, can love no creature on the face of the earth for its own sake, but only in the Creator of them all. It is likewise consolation when one sheds tears that move to the love of God, whether it be because of sorrow for sins, or because of the sufferings of Christ our Lord....Finally, I call consolation every increase of faith, hope, and love...filling [the soul] with peace and quiet in its Creator and Lord.

SPIRITUAL EXERCISE, NO. 316

THE SPIRITUAL EXERCISES OF ST. IGNATIUS, 142

"HAVING LOVED HIS OWN,"
HE WASHED HIS DISCIPLES' FEET

Now before the festival of the Passover, Jesus knew that his hour had come to depart from this world and go to the Father. Having loved his own who were in the world, he loved them to the end. [Jesus] got up from the table…poured water into a basin and began to wash the disciples' feet.…

After he had washed their feet…and had returned to the table, he said to them, "Do you know what I have done to you? You call me Teacher and Lord—and you are right, for that is what I am. So if I, your Lord and Teacher, have washed your feet, you also ought to wash one another's feet. For I have set you an example, that you also should do as I have done to you."

JOHN 13:1, 4–5, 12–15

PRAYER

Lord, help me to imagine you, to see you, washing my feet with your cleansing, healing, forgiving love every day, every moment, of my life. Open my eyes to see you down on your knees in front of me, washcloth in hand, gently massaging my feet. And fill me with amazement and gratitude for your care for me. This I ask through Christ our Lord, Amen.

LENTEN ACTION

Think of a person or two for whom you are an "authority figure"—as Jesus was "Teacher and Lord" of the apostles—and imagine a way in which your treatment of them could, quite casually, be a "foot washing." Isn't that what servant leadership is like?

DAY 45

He Gave Up His Spirit

WHAT HAVE I, AM I, OUGHT I...FOR CHRIST?

Imagine Christ our Lord present before you upon the cross, and begin to speak with him, asking how it is that though He is the Creator, He has stooped to become man, and to pass from eternal life to death here in time, that thus He might die for our sins.

I shall also reflect upon myself and ask:

"What have I done for Christ?"

"What am I doing for Christ?"

"What ought I to do for Christ?"

As I behold Christ in this plight, nailed to the cross, I shall ponder upon what presents itself to my mind.

SPIRITUAL EXERCISE, NO. 53

THE SPIRITUAL EXERCISES OF ST. IGNATIUS, 28

"HERE IS YOUR MOTHER"

...Meanwhile, standing near the cross of Jesus were his mother, and his mother's sister, Mary the wife of Clopas, and Mary Magdalene. When Jesus saw his mother and the disciple whom he loved standing beside her, he said to his mother, "Woman, here is your son." Then he said to the disciple, "Here is your mother." And from that hour the disciple took her into his own home.

After this, when Jesus knew that all was now finished, he said (in order to fulfil the scripture), "I am thirsty." A jar full of sour wine was standing there. So they put a sponge full of the wine on a branch of hyssop and held it to his mouth. When Jesus had received the wine, he said, "It is finished." Then he bowed his head and gave up his spirit.

JOHN 19:25–30

PRAYER

Dear Lord, thank you for giving us Mary, your Mother, as our model for responding to you and joining our hearts with you in your loving death for us—even as your enemies ridiculed and brutalized you. May the breath of your Spirit fill my heart now as it filled Mary's heart beneath your cross. Amen.

LENTEN ACTION

Karl Rahner, the great Catholic German theologian, says that Jesus' death, resurrection, and ascension all happened simultaneously on the cross. Imagine how Mary, as she joined her heart with her dying son's death, was also being filled with the joy of eternal life. How proud she was of her son!

DAY 46

The Women at the Empty Tomb

THE RISEN CHRIST APPEARING TO HIS MOTHER—FIRST

*T*he apparition of Christ our Lord to our Lady....[A]fter Christ expired on the cross His body remained separated from the soul, but always united with the divinity. His soul, likewise united with the divinity, descended into hell. There he sets free the souls of the just, then comes to the sepulcher, and rising, appears in body and soul to His Blessed Mother.

...[A]sk for the grace to be glad and rejoice intensely because of the great joy and the glory of Christ our Lord.

Consider the office of consoler that Christ our Lord exercises with the way in which friends are wont to console each other.

SPIRITUAL EXERCISES, NOS. 219, 221, 224
THE SPIRITUAL EXERCISES OF ST. IGNATIUS, 95–96

AND THEN TO THE OTHER WOMEN

...[O]n the first day of the week, at early dawn, they came to the tomb, taking the spices that they had prepared. They found the stone rolled away from the tomb, but when they went in, they did not find the body. While they were perplexed about this, suddenly two men in dazzling clothes stood beside them. The women were terrified and bowed their faces to the ground, but the men said to them, "Why do you look for the living among the dead? He is not here, but has risen. Remember how he told you, while he was still in Galilee, that the Son of Man must be handed over to sinners, and be crucified, and on the third day rise again." Then they remembered his words...

LUKE 24:1–8

PRAYER

Lord Jesus, now risen through death to new life, please open my mind to grasp gratefully and move my heart to embrace joyfully your presence with us now and forever. Inspire me to share this Good News with all I meet. Amen.

LENTEN ACTION

Some people said to Ignatius, "There is no evidence that Jesus appeared to Mary first." Ponder Ignatius' witty response (in the Spiritual Exercise, No. 299): "...[I]t must be considered as stated when Scripture says that He appeared to many others. For Scripture supposes that we have understanding, as it is written, 'Are you also without understanding?'"

PART II

~~~~~~

READINGS *for* EASTER

DAY 47

EASTER SUNDAY

"Love Manifests Itself in Deeds"

THE CONTEMPLATION TO ATTAIN THE LOVE OF GOD

The first [point] is that love ought to manifest itself in deeds rather than in words.

The second is that love consists in a mutual sharing of goods, for example, the lover gives and shares with the beloved what he possesses, or something of that which he has or is able to give; and vice versa....Thus, one always gives to the other.

SPIRITUAL EXERCISES, NOS. 230–231
THE SPIRITUAL EXERCISES OF ST. IGNATIUS, 101

MARY MAGDALENE, SIMON PETER, AND THE OTHER DISCIPLE WHOM JESUS LOVED

[Mary Magdalene] went to Simon Peter and the other disciple, the one whom Jesus loved, and said to them, "They have taken the Lord out of the tomb, and we do not know where they have laid him." Then Peter and the other disciple set out and went towards the tomb. He bent down to look in and saw the linen wrappings lying there, but he did not go in. Then Simon Peter came, following him, and went into the tomb. He saw the linen wrappings lying there, and the cloth that had been on Jesus' head, not lying with the linen wrappings but rolled up in a place by itself. Then the other disciple, who reached the tomb first, also went in, and he saw and believed; for as yet they did not understand the scripture, that he must rise from the dead.

JOHN 20:2–3, 5–9

PRAYER

Lord, inspire me with the courage, the devotion, and the energy of Mary Magdalene, who was the first witness to others—even to the Apostles themselves—of your resurrection. Never let fear of ridicule or rejection block me from living openly and sharing warmly the Good News I know! Amen.

EASTER ACTION

"Love consists in a mutual sharing of goods," Ignatius says. Share with several others today your faith, joy, and appreciation for the life-giving gift of Jesus' death and resurrection.

DAY 48

EASTER MONDAY

The Story to This Day

"I WILL PONDER WITH GREAT AFFECTION HOW MUCH GOD HAS DONE FOR ME"

This is to ask for what I desire…an intimate knowledge of the many blessings received, that filled with gratitude for all, I may in all things love and serve the Divine Majesty. [I] recall…to mind the blessings of creation and redemption, and the special favors I have received.

I will ponder with great affection how much God has done for me, and how much He has given me of what He possesses, and finally, how much, as far as he can, the same Lord desires to give of Himself to me according to His divine decrees.

SPIRITUAL EXERCISES, NOS. 233–234
THE SPIRITUAL EXERCISES OF ST. IGNATIUS, 101–102

"HIS DISCIPLES CAME BY NIGHT AND STOLE HIM AWAY..."

So [the women] left the tomb quickly with fear and great joy, and ran to tell his disciples.

While they were going, some of the guard went into the city and told the chief priests everything that had happened. After the priests had assembled with the elders, they devised a plan to give a large sum of money to the soldiers, telling them, "You must say, 'His disciples came by night and stole him away while we were asleep.' If this comes to the governor's ears, we will satisfy him and keep you out of trouble." So they took the money and did as they were directed. And this story is still told among the Jews to this day.

MATTHEW 28:8, 11–15

PRAYER

Lord, no sooner had you fully poured out upon us your love, forgiveness, and promise of continuing care, than some people started lying about you and your friends. The priests concocted deceit, and the guards were bribed. Teach me, as you taught your Apostles, to be "wise as serpents and innocent as doves" (Matthew 10:16), as I carry your message of love, hope, and unity to our world. Amen.

EASTER ACTION

Spend some time recording in your journal some of the great blessings you have received in the course of your life, ultimately from God, but normally mediated through family, friends, and many others. Keep this list handy, because recalling our gifts is a good way to start a period of prayer at any time.

DAY 49

"Mary!" "Rabbouni!"

"I WILL MAKE THIS OFFERING OF MYSELF"

*T*hen I will reflect…what I ought to offer the Divine Majesty, that is, all I possess and myself with it. Thus, as one would do who is moved by great feeling, I will make this offering of myself:

Take, Lord, and receive all my liberty, my memory, my understanding, and my entire will, all that 1 have and possess. Thou hast given all to me. To Thee, O Lord, I return it. All is Thine, dispose of it wholly according to Thy will. Give me Thy love and Thy grace, for this is sufficient for me.

SPIRITUAL EXERCISE, NO. 234

THE SPIRITUAL EXERCISES OF ST. IGNATIUS, 102

"WHY ARE YOU WEEPING?"

But Mary stood weeping outside the tomb. As she wept, she bent over to look into the tomb; and she saw two angels in white, sitting where the body of Jesus had been lying...They said to her, "Woman, why are you weeping?" She said to them, "They have taken away my Lord, and I do not know where they have laid him." When she had said this, she turned round and saw Jesus standing there, but she did not know that it was Jesus. Jesus said to her, "Woman, why are you weeping? For whom are you looking?" Supposing him to be the gardener, she said to him, "Sir, if you have carried him away, tell me where you have laid him, and I will take him away." Jesus said to her, "Mary!" She turned and said to him in Hebrew, "Rabbouni!" (which means Teacher).

JOHN 20:11–16

PRAYER

Lord, move my heart to tears of joy and gratitude, when like Mary, I hear you utter my name and call me to join you in your continuing mission of love and reconciliation in our world. Amen.

EASTER ACTION

Put your fingers on your wrist and feel your pulse beat—the rhythm of life. Hear each beat as the voice of Jesus uttering your name over and over.

DAY 50

EASTER WEDNESDAY

"Were Not Our Hearts Burning Within Us?..."

GOD DWELLS IN ME, HIS TEMPLE

*R*eflect how God dwells in creatures: in the elements giving them existence, in the plants giving them life, in the animals conferring upon them sensation, in [humans] bestowing understanding. So He dwells in me and gives me being, life, sensation, intelligence; and makes a temple of me, since I am created in the likeness and image of the Divine Majesty.

Then I will reflect upon myself again in the manner stated in the first point....

SPIRITUAL EXERCISE, NO. 235
THE SPIRITUAL EXERCISES OF ST. IGNATIUS, 102

"Were Not Our Hearts Burning Within Us?..."

...[T]wo of them were going to a village called Emmaus....While they were talking and discussing, Jesus himself came near and went with them, but their eyes were kept from recognizing him. Then he said to them,..."Was it not necessary that the Messiah should suffer these things and then enter into his glory?" Then beginning with Moses and all the prophets, he interpreted to them the things about himself in all the scriptures. When he was at the table with them, he took bread, blessed and broke it, and gave it to them. Then their eyes were opened, and they recognized him; and he vanished from their sight. They said to each other, "Were not our hearts burning within us while he was talking to us on the road, while he was opening the scriptures to us?"

LUKE 24:13–16, 25–27, 30–32

Prayer

Lord, when I attend Mass, help me to hear the Scripture as your voice speaking to the disciples on the road to Emmaus; help my heart to burn with gratitude at the breaking of bread. Amen.

Easter Action

Sometime today sit down and read the whole Gospel story of Jesus joining the disciples on the way to Emmaus. Imagine yourself as a third disciple in the group, listening to Jesus. Notice the tone of his voice.

DAY 51

EASTER THURSDAY

You Are Witnesses of These Things

GOD AS ONE WHO LABORS

*C*onsider how God works and labors for me in all creatures upon the face of the earth, that is, He conducts Himself as one who labors. Thus, in the heavens, the elements, the plants, the fruits, the cattle, etc., He gives being, conserves them, confers life and sensation, etc.

...[C]onsider all blessings and gifts as descending from above. Thus, my limited power comes from the supreme and infinite power above, and so, too, justice, goodness, mercy, etc., descend from above as the rays of light descend from the sun, and as the waters flow from their fountains, etc.

Then I will reflect on myself [and consider what I ought to offer the Divine Majesty].

SPIRITUAL EXERCISES, NOS. 236–237
THE SPIRITUAL EXERCISES OF ST. IGNATIUS, 103

TOUCH ME AND SEE

While [the apostles] were talking about this, Jesus himself stood among them and said to them, "Peace be with you." They were startled and terrified, and thought that they were seeing a ghost. He said to them, "Why are you frightened, and why do doubts arise in your hearts? Look at my hands and my feet; see that it is I myself. Touch me and see; for a ghost does not have flesh and bones as you see that I have." Then he opened their minds to understand the scriptures, and he said to them, "Thus it is written, that the Messiah is to suffer and to rise from the dead on the third day, and that repentance and forgiveness of sins is to be proclaimed in his name to all nations, beginning from Jerusalem. You are witnesses of these things."

LUKE 24:36–39, 45–48

PRAYER

Lord, let me touch you in mind, imagination, and heart as you give yourself to me as my life, as my intelligence, as my yearning, and as my desire to love others. And help me to say "Thanks!" Amen.

EASTER ACTION

Go out for a walk and look at trees, grass, clouds, people, and cars moving. Feel the breeze on your brow. And know that all this vitality is God present, laboring, and sustaining in love.

DAY 52

EASTER FRIDAY

"It Is the Lord!"

DEDICATION TO THE LORD'S SERVICE

We give thanks to God for this ineffable mercy and kindness with which He overwhelms us through the power of His glorious name. I am deeply moved when I hear or behold with my own eyes the work which you and others who are called to the Society are accomplishing in Christ Jesus.

Courage, then, courage!...The same Lord it is who worketh in us both to will and to accomplish, according to His good will.... For the Spirit of Jesus will give thee in all things understanding and fortitude, to the end that through you the name of Jesus will be glorified....

LETTERS OF ST. IGNATIUS OF LOYOLA
"TO PETER CANISIUS," 97

CAST YOUR NET TO THE STARBOARD!

Simon Peter said to them, "I am going fishing." [The others] said to him, "We will go with you." They went out and got into the boat, but that night they caught nothing.

Just after daybreak, Jesus stood on the beach; but the disciples did not know that it was Jesus. Jesus said to them, "Children, you have no fish, have you?" They answered him, "No." He said to them, "Cast the net to the right side of the boat, and you will find some." So they cast it, and now they were not able to haul it in because there were so many fish. That disciple whom Jesus loved said to Peter, "It is the Lord!"...This was now the third time that Jesus appeared to the disciples after he was raised from the dead.

JOHN 21: 3–7, 14

PRAYER

Lord, I want to dedicate myself, my life, to your service by serving the good of others in my life. But without you, I am unable. Let me hear your word, "Cast your net," and let it empower me to serve well. Amen.

EASTER ACTION

Recall and reflect on "net fishing." The Apostles never "pole fished." How is net fishing symbolic of our mission to gather people and forge community in our world?

DAY 53

<small>EASTER SATURDAY</small>

Incredulous Apostles—
Called to Spread Faith

FREE—TO PRAISE AND SERVE GOD

*Y*ou ask me for the love of God our Lord to undertake the direction of your soul....

I will be very glad to give you a frank opinion; and if at times I appear severe, it will be rather against him who is trying to upset you than against you yourself. The enemy is leading you into error in two things....In the first place he proposes and leads you on to a false humility. And in the second, he gives you an exaggerated fear of God, with which you are altogether too much occupied.

LETTERS OF ST. IGNATIUS OF LOYOLA
"TO SISTER TERESA REJADELL," 19

APPARITIONS...LEADING TO...COMMISSION

Now after he rose early on the first day of the week, he appeared first to Mary Magdalene....She went out and told those who had been with him...[but] they would not believe it.

After this he appeared in another form to two of them, as they were walking into the country. And they went back and told the rest, but they did not believe them.

Later he appeared to the eleven themselves as they were sitting at the table; and he upbraided them for their lack of faith and stubbornness, because they had not believed those who saw him after he had risen. And he said to them, "Go into all the world and proclaim the good news to the whole creation."

MARK 16: 9–15

PRAYER

Lord, give me the personal freedom and willingness to acknowledge the lack of faith and the stubbornness which I share with your first disciples and apostles, because only then, I know, will your healing touch be able to reach me and enable me to share your love and desires with others. Amen.

EASTER ACTION

Read again during the day the citation above from Saint Ignatius. Are the temptations of Sister Teresa also your temptations? If not, what does trap your freedom? Look for that trap in your daily Examination of Conscience, as described in Day 21.

DAY 54

FIRST SUNDAY AFTER EASTER

Living and Sharing the Life of Christ's Spirit

"LOVE ONE ANOTHER AS I HAVE LOVED YOU"

*I*t is this obedience that I recommend very earnestly to you, joined with that virtue which is a compendium of all the others and which Jesus Christ so earnestly recommends when He calls it His especial commandment: "This is my commandment, that you love one another" (John 15:12). And I wish that you preserve this union and lasting love, not only among yourselves, but that you extend it to all, and endeavor to enkindle in your souls the lively desire for the salvation of your neighbor, gauging the value of each soul from the price our Lord paid of His Life's blood.

LETTERS OF ST. IGNATIUS OF LOYOLA
"TO THE FATHERS AND SCHOLASTICS AT COIMBRA," 128

FORGIVENESS RECEIVED AND SHARED

When it was evening on that day, the first day of the week, and the doors of the house where the disciples had met were locked for fear of the Jews, Jesus came and stood among them and said, "Peace be with you." After he said this, he showed them his hands and his side. Then the disciples rejoiced when they saw the Lord. Jesus said to them again, "Peace be with you. As the Father has sent me, so I send you." When he had said this, he breathed on them and said to them, "Receive the Holy Spirit. If you forgive the sins of any, they are forgiven them; if you retain the sins of any, they are retained."

...[T]hese [signs] are written so that...you may have life in his name.

JOHN 20:19–23, 30–31

PRAYER

Lord, you send us as you sent your first Apostles on a mission of offering forgiveness and reconciliation to others "that all may be one." To do so, we need to be living out the gift of your forgiveness and the life of your Spirit. Help me, Lord, to know this well and to live it fully. Amen.

EASTER ACTION

Take a few minutes to record in your journal the five insights, feelings, or experiences that were most influential for you on this journey through Lent and Easter with Jesus and Ignatius.

Acknowledgments

Letters of St. Ignatius of Loyola. Translated by William J. Young, SJ. Chicago: Loyola University Press, 1959. © 1959 Loyola University Press. Used by permission of Loyola Press.

St. Ignatius' Own Story. Translated by William J. Young, SJ. Chicago: Loyola University Press, 1980. © 1980 Loyola University Press. Used by permission of Loyola Press.

The Constitutions of the Society of Jesus and Their Complementary Norms: A Complete English Translation of the Official Latin Texts. St. Louis: The Institute of Jesuit Sources, 1996. Used by permission of The Institute of Jesuit Sources.

The Spiritual Exercises of St. Ignatius. Translated by Louis J. Puhl, SJ. Chicago: Loyola University Press, 1951. © 1951 by The Newman Press. Used by permission of Loyola Press.